Don't You Laugh at Me!

Story by Joy Cowley

Spider is laughing.

"Don't you laugh at me," says Bird, "or I'll eat you."

But Spider can't stop laughing.

So Bird eats him.

Now Bird can't stop laughing.

"Don't you laugh at me," says Cat, "or I'll eat you."

But Bird can't stop laughing.

So Cat eats her.

Now Cat can't stop laughing.

"Don't you laugh at me," says Dog, "or I'll eat you."

But Cat can't stop laughing.

So Dog eats him.

Now Dog can't stop laughing.

"Don't you laugh at me," says Tiger, "or I'll eat you."

But Dog can't stop laughing.

So Tiger eats her.

Now Tiger can't stop laughing.

"Don't you laugh at me,"
says Alligator, "or I'll eat you."

But Tiger can't stop laughing.

So Alligator eats him.

Now Alligator can't stop laughing.
"Ha, ha, ha! Ho, ho, ho!"

She laughs so hard,
she gets the hiccups.

Hup! Up comes Tiger.
Hup! Up comes Dog.

Hup! Up comes Cat.
Hup! Up comes Bird.
Hup! Up comes Spider.

And they all go down
the road, laughing.